1-2-3 Family Tree

The fastest way to create and grow your family tree from the leading family history company, MyFamily.com.

Guide to Building Your Family Tree

1-2-3 Family Tree
P.O. Box 476
Salt Lake City, Utah 84110-0476
1-800-ANCESTRY

ISBN: 1-931279-17-9

Library of Congress catalog card number
1-2-3 family tree / by MyFamily.com, Inc.
p. cm.
Includes bibliographical references.
ISBN 1-931279-17-9 (pbk. : alk. paper)
1. Genealogy. 2. United States--Genealogy--Handbooks, manuals, etc.
I. Title: 123 family tree. II. Title: One-two-three family tree. III.
MyFamily.com, Inc.
CS16 .A15 2002
929'.1'072073--dc21
2002000874

NOTE: MyFamily.com, Inc. is the leading provider of family history resource information and tools on the Web.
Ancestry.com is a genealogical Web site owned by MyFamily.com, Inc.

Table of Contents

1-2-3 Family Tree

Welcome to the *1-2-3 Family Tree* Guide. You are about to embark on an adventure; one that is exciting, rewarding, and easier than ever with the help of modern-day advances such as computers and the Internet. *1-2-3 Family Tree* will teach you three steps that will get you well on your way to discovering your ancestors. With the information and research tools you will learn about in this guide you can create a personal family tree that will bring you unparalleled knowledge about who you are today. Enjoy the adventure!

STEP ONE
Learning the 5 Ws of Detective Work

IN STEP ONE YOU WILL:

- Record your personal information in genealogical software

- Extend the information in your family tree to your parents and grandparents

- Conduct an interview with a relative

- Learn to write an effective letter

- Query electronically using the Internet

Any good detective knows that the key to an investigation is learning *The Five Ws*– Who, What, When, Where, and Why. They are simple words—not one of them is over five letters long. However, in those five words you will find the key to becoming a great detective, and being a detective is exactly what you are when you do family history. Take for instance the story of Bonnie, a woman working in a genealogical research center in Seattle, Washington.

The Passport

On a slower than normal afternoon, Bonnie, an amateur genealogist who volunteered her time at a local genealogical center, decided to clean out the box labeled "Lost and Found." While cleaning, Bonnie came across a plastic bag that contained a Swedish sailor's passport and some old postcards. The man in the passport had been born in 1908. Other than that, there was only the name of a woman, whose given name was Ann, scribbled on the outside of the plastic bag.

From asking around, Bonnie found out that the bag had been found near one of the center's microfilm readers about five years back. Workers had tried to contact the owner of the bag with no luck. The items had sat in the "Lost and Found" for half a decade. Bonnie got an idea. Instead of just throwing the items away, she decided she would track down the owner.

To begin, she did what anyone would do. She looked up Ann's name in the phone book. Nothing. Next, she actually drove to the Seattle address on the old postcards. Again, nothing. Then Bonnie's skills in genealogy began to kick in.

Bonnie began using records and information that you will learn about in this guide to uncover a living descendant of the man in the passport. First, she went to the 1920 Federal Census records and looked up that same address that was on the postcards. She discovered that in 1920 that address was the home of the man named in the Swedish passport. He had two daughters, one named Ann.

That led Bonnie to Seattle's Polk city directories (similar directories can be found in most large cities). Using them, she followed the family through the years. Eventually, the family no longer lived at the address on the postcards. Ann, with a married name (the one on the plastic bag) appeared at a new residence. Coles city directories revealed the current owners of this second residence. A telephone call to these people produced the current residence of Ann's daughter.

When Bonnie contacted Ann's daughter to see if she would like her grandfather's belongings, she was thrilled, and Bonnie felt the exhilaration of a detective job well done.

Gathering Your Own 5 Ws

The first Five Ws that you should gather are your own. Using Chart #1, record the following information:

1. Write your name **(who).**

2. Write **what** important events you've had in your life (e.g., birth, christening, baptism, education, marriage, etc).

3. Write **where** each of the events took place (the city, county, state, country, or providence).

4. Write **when** each specific event took place.

5. Write **why** you know these things happened. In other words, write the evidence that shows everyone else that these events really took place (e.g., church records, school admissions, government records, etc.).

You have just started your family tree. Now, since genealogy is really just a collection of individuals, their life events, as well as their relation to each other, you should keep going. After compiling information about yourself, start on your parents' Five Ws, and then move on to their parents. If you don't know all of the Five Ws about a person, just leave a blank and go as far as you can. Record this information on Chart #2. The following list gives you more detail about the Five Ws.

Chart #1 –Personal Profile

Full Name: _____

Birth Date: _____

Birth Place: _____
_____
_____

Religious Events: _____
_____
_____
_____

Education: _____
_____
_____
_____

Marriage: _____
_____

Children: _____
_____
_____
_____

Miscellaneous: _____
_____
_____
_____
_____
_____
_____
_____

Who: Write the person's full name, including all middle names and any titles that might be relevant (Rev., Capt., Dr.). If you don't have the full name, don't worry. Include as much as you do know. Write a female's name using her family or birth name, not her married name. If you only know her married name, then write this in parentheses [e.g., Mary (Jones)]. This will serve as a visual reminder that you need to research further into her identity. Record any nicknames.

What: Identify the event as clearly as possible. For example, when listing graduation as an event in a person's life, specify which level of graduation is being documented (e.g., high school, college). Use abbreviations for events (e.g., b for birth or bap for baptism). These abbreviations should be consistent.

Where: Record as much as you know about the location of a particular event. For example, a birth may have occurred in a hospital. When recording the location of this birth, name the hospital, town or city, county, state, province (if applicable), and even the country if necessary. It's quicker to use abbreviations for place names such as ME for Maine or FL for Florida. Remember to be consistent.

When: As you write dates in your family history, use the international method of date entry, which puts the day first, then the standard three-letter abbreviation for the month, and then all four digits for the year. For example, October 11, 1884 or 10/11/1884 is written as 10 OCT 1884.

Why (evidence): As you gather information—from a conversation, a family Bible, a treasured letter, a birth certificate, or a published family history—record the source as thoroughly as possible. Documentation is necessary for others to judge the reliability and accuracy of your work. If you keep a list of your sources, that list could serve as a bibliography for a finished project such as a book. The Ancestry Family Tree software has a specific place to record source information. You will learn more about this software and how to record sources in the next section.

Chart #2 – Parents and Grandparents Information

Mother's Name: _____

Father's Name: _____

Mother's Birth Place: _____
Birth Date: _____

Father's Birth Place: _____
Birth Date: _____

Parent's Marriage Information*: _____
_____

Parent's Death Information*: _____
_____

Miscellaneous: _____
_____

Grandmother's Name: _____

Grandfather's Name: _____

Grandmother's Birth Place: _____
Birth Date: _____

Grandfather's Birth Place: _____
Birth Date: _____

Grandparent's Marriage Information*: _____
_____

Grandparent's Death Information*: _____
_____

Miscellaneous: _____

* *if applicable*

Creating Your First Family Tree

After writing down as many of the Five Ws that you know about yourself, your parents, your grandparents, and maybe even their parents, you will notice that you have blanks appearing more and more frequently. Don't be discouraged. There are some very quick and easy ways you will soon learn to help you fill in those blanks.

Before going any further, you must learn how to organize the information you are collecting. Recording your research is simple through the use of computers. This guide relies on the *Ancestry Family Tree* software as the method to record your research. Read the following section to help you quickly learn the basic steps of recording information in *Ancestry Family Tree*.

3" x 5" cards can be a means of recording information on the individuals in your family tree. Each card represents a new person. His or her name is written at the top with the important information listed below. Evidence of the research can be placed on the back of the card.

The pedigree chart is one of the most easily recognized forms used by genealogists. In this chart you can show relationships between multiple generations of a family and trace your ancestry back in time along a particular family line. A pedigree only shows you ancestors. There is no room on a pedigree chart for siblings, multiple marriages, or social family connections. This information appears on a different form.

The Family group sheet or family group record allows you to enter all the individuals connected to a particular family. At the top there is space for the names and vital information on the husband (or father) and wife (or mother). There is space for the names of all the children born to the union of the two people named at the top

A research log is where you record the sources you have consulted and the information you were seeking. By being diligent in working on this form, you will save yourself countless hours of retracing your steps.

The *Ancestry Family Tree* software incorporates all of these methods of recording keeping.

Ancestry Family Tree Record Keeping

To install *Ancestry Family Tree*, place the CD into your CD drive and follow the on-screen, step-by-step instructions. Once the software is loaded, you can start inputting the information from Charts #1 and #2.

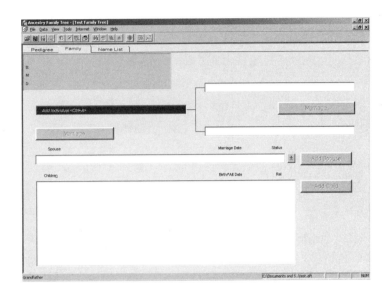

On the main screen of Ancestry Family Tree, you will see three tabs "Pedigree; Family; Name List." Click on "Pedigree." This page allows you to view a five-generation pedigree chart at one time. Click the first generation field where it says "Add 1st Person." This will bring up a new window entitled "Add New Individual." Using the information from Chart #1, fill in all of the information about yourself that you can. (Note: This window will allow you to input information about yourself and about the rest of your family elsewhere.)

If you have additional information about events in your life, click on the "More" button at the bottom of the window. To record notes about certain events, click on the "Notes" button at the bottom of the page. To record the source for a particular event, click on the "S" button to the right of the "Place" field. Use the "Help" button if you have questions about how to add the source information.

Once you have finished recording information about yourself, you are ready to add family information. Click the "Save" button. This will take you back to the "Pedigree" page. Then, click on the tab "Family." This page allows you to input information about your marriage, your parents, and your children. This is the connecting page. It connects you to a family and your family to you. To add a spouse, click on the "Spouse" field. To record the date and place of your marriage, click on the "Marriage" button. Likewise, click on the "Mother/Father" fields to input their names, and click on the "Marriage" button by their fields to enter their marriage information. Input the names of any children you have in the "Children" field. To get back to the "Pedigree" page, make sure your name is in the "Root Person" field and then simply click on the tab "Pedigree." The tab "Name List" shows a listing of all of the names you have entered so far.

You have just used the basic features of the *Ancestry Family Tree* software. There are more features, and the more you move about in the software, the more you will learn. For example, Ancestry Family Tree offers a direct link to the databases on the genealogical Web site Ancestry.com. Ancestry.com is a part of MyFamily.com, the company that produced *1-2-3 Family Tree*. The Ancestry.com Web site and the feature to link directly from *Ancestry Family Tree* to Ancestry.com will be explained further in STEP TWO.

Also in Ancestry Family Tree there is way to create a "Descendancy List." A Descendancy List displays the names and birth dates of parents, siblings, spouse(s), and children of a Selected Individual. You can also attach a photo or sound clip of an individual through the "Media" button. You can import/export genealogical files, and there is a function to help you quickly search through data. Use the menu item "Help" to find on-screen answers to questions you may have.

Clues to the Past

Once you have recorded the information you knew from memory, you are ready to expand your search to include any information that is close at hand. STEP ONE covers ways to quickly start filling up your family tree. STEPS TWO and THREE discuss more involved methods that can help you trace your ancestry back centuries.

Your first item of business is to look for clues to your past within your home or within the homes of relatives. Take a look around any storage rooms or attics for some of the following items. If you have nothing in your own home, that may mean you get to take a weekend vacation to your parents. You may decide to call your great aunt whom you have been meaning to visit anyway. While visiting, ask about and look around for some of the following valuable home resources.

 Letters: Some families have carefully saved letters. These letters may yield some valuable insight into the relationships of your family members. Even if they have no genealogical information, letters provide unique insights.

 **Scrapbooks:** Some of the most interesting and useful information can be found in these mementos. While scrapbooks may not contain direct genealogical evidence, they do provide documentation of certain events, and they add wonderful anecdotes to a family history.

 **Military memorabilia:** Military records are a major source of genealogical data and will be covered in length in a later section. Along with records are military memorabilia that includes things that have been saved because of some unique or emotional value. Items such as group pictures, weapons, uniforms, or unit histories place an individual at a particular place and time.

School records: School-related records may prove valuable. Examples include report cards, registration papers that name parents, school yearbooks, a student essay written by your relative, certificates of achievement, diplomas, etc.

Licenses: An old driver's license, a professional license, or a hunting/fishing license could all make for interesting sources.

Keepsakes: Some potentially helpful items may not be stored away but are actually prominently displayed in a home. Jewelry, passed down from parent to child, may have engravings that provide valuable clues about the owner. Likewise, check out all furniture built by an ancestor. Inspect mirrors for a generation of ownership inscribed on the back. There are numerous other examples of useful household items that are valuable to the genealogist.

Genealogy is all about clues, and there is no better place to start looking for these clues than in the home. This list contains only a few suggestions. Be creative and don't forget to ask questions. Imagine what might be around your home, utilize what you have, and keep records. Consider the following story told by Terry and Jim Willard. They found generations of information resting in dusty boxes of an old basement.

Treasures in the Attic

Since we had no real genealogical treasures in our home, we began our search by taking a short trip to Jim's parent's home.

I began with a telephone conversation in 1968. While talking with Jim's mother about our new hobby, we asked if she might have any information at her home that wold be useful. Specifically, we were hoping there might be an old family bible with names and dates hand written on the inside jacket. We were taking a local history course as part of our undergraduate studies and our professor, an amateur genealogist, indicated that a family Bible was one of the real treasures of family history. Any student whose family had one would get a bonus grade. She told us there was no family bible, but that there were two boxes in the basement.

We spent four rewarding hours poring over the contents of those two boxes. The contents of the boxes had been divided between family sides, so items from Jim's father's family were in one and items from Jim's mother's family were in the other. In the box containing records of Jim's paternal family, the first items that proved useful were birth certificates of his grandparents. These documents yielded another generation of names. In addition, the place of birth was given which provided a valuable clue to the marriage location of their parents. A second major find was Jim's great-grandfather's will. It named his wife, all of his children, and the location of his home and property. It also named two more people in a preceding generation, filling in more of the blanks on his pedigree chart.

We also discovered Jim's grandfather's handwritten business ledger, used for one of the businesses he had owned in his lifetime, and Jim's father's high school report cards. While these documents provided no genealogical information, they did give us insight into the personalities of these men. The final items in Jim's paternal keepsake box included property deeds, old newspaper clippings containing articles of interest to the family, military discharge papers, and, of course, pictures.

The box containing items from Jim's mother's family proved equally rewarding. Perhaps the most significant find in the maternal storage box was his grandfather's application for naturalization. His application listed his full name, wife's name, living children, occupation, date and place of birth (the most significant clue), and signature. This one document told us more about Jim's grandparents than we knew up to that point, and ultimately led us to several more generations of information.

There were also some religious items that provided clues for us to follow. Among these were burial mass cards—small documents, similar to obituaries that are distributed at the funeral mass held for the individual. Other helpful items of a religious nature were baptismal, confirmation, and marriage certificates. One other item of note in the box was a train ticket. While seemingly unimportant at first, it turned out to be a ticket purchased by Jim's grandparents for their honeymoon trip to Old Orchard Beach, Maine, just after the turn of the century. It so happened that Jim's grandfather got off the train while it was stopped for water about sixty miles from their destination. He responded to an advertisement for employment, took the job, and secured housing for he and his bride—they didn't continue any further. Forty years and sixteen children later, they finally made it to Old Orchard.

Living Sources

A good detective would never let an investigation end until he or she had interviewed all of the witnesses to an event. You should be the same way when finding information to fill in blanks on your family tree. Talking to a living source is a valuable key in the formation of a family tree as seen in the story of Lorie.

Grandma's Door

Lorie was intensely nervous as she knocked at the strange door in Vienna. She had met her grandmother only once, and had found her frightening, stern, and opinionated. Lorie had written with apprehension to ask if she could visit Grandmother Rosa in Vienna to learn details about her mother's childhood. Lorie's mom, who had died when Lorie was thirty-one, had rarely spoken of her growing-up years. She had left no diaries or journals.

Since her mother's death, a yearning had grown within Lorie to know and understand her mother. Lorie had started her quest by writing and phoning her brothers and sisters. This did not yield much. Next Lorie wrote to her mother's old friends in Austria and America. From this she got a few more stories, but not enough. Finally she realized that only her Grandmother Rosa knew the details of her mother's childhood.

As little as Lorie knew about her mother, she knew even less about her grandmother. The one thing Lorie knew for sure about her grandmother was that she had been strict and scary. Consequently, she trembled in front of Rosa's door. The door opened to show a very small woman with a firm, resolute mouth, her hair covered with a bandanna.

"So! You are finally here! Come in! Come in!"

After she fed Lorie a fine dinner, Rosa finally asked, "Now, what was it you wanted to ask me?"

Lorie replied, "I wanted to have you tell me about my mother's childhood. I know nothing about it, and she rarely spoke of it. I thought you would know the details."

Rosa, puzzled, then incensed, blurted out, "Your mother's childhood? Why, her childhood was nothing!" She gave a dismissive wave of her hand. "Now *my* childhood! That was something! I'll tell you!"

And tell her she did. Rosa spoke without pause for nearly three hours, relating stories that were almost unbelievable. Lorie returned over the next three days, and again the next year. She recorded many hours of detailed information concerning her mother and grandmother's lives. She had never suspected that her knock on her grandmother's door would begin an adventure that added unimaginable richness to her life.

The Gatekeeper

Usually at least one person in every family, sometimes referred to as a gatekeeper, knows a significant amount of that family's history. These people are perhaps the best source of a family's genealogical information. If you don't think there is a gatekeeper in your family, there are ways to gather information from family members even if they feel they know little about the family's history. There are even methods of gathering information from people who are not members of your family.

There are three basic methods of collecting information from living sources. These methods are:

1. personal interviewing

2. letter writing

3. querying

Any or all of these methods can be used to track down information.

Interview Questions

Where did you live as a child?
What are your most vivid childhood memories?
Were you close to any of your grandparents?
If so, what are your favorite memories of them?
What was the most serious illness you had as a child?
What do you remember best about your grade school years?
What did you do as a child that got you in the most trouble?
How did your parents handle it?
What were your mother's best and worst traits?
Which of these traits do you share with your mother?
What were your father's best and worst traits?
Which of these traits do you share with your father?
What do you remember best about your brothers and sisters?
In what ways did they influence your growing up years?
What stories do you remember about things you did with them?
Was religion important in your home?
If so, what practices made it important?
Did you have a favorite uncle or aunt?
What do you best remember about them?
Which of your neighbors were memorable?
What stories do you remember about them?
Was junior high a hard transition time?
What activities did you love most in high school?
How well do remember your first real romance?
What was your most embarrassing moment?
What things do you enjoy doing today that you also enjoyed in your youth?
What things do you remember about being a teenager?
What was important to you then—dreams, goals, etc.?
What family traditions do you still remember?
What holidays were special in your family?
What did you do to celebrate them?
What do you remember about your first job?
How much did you make and how did you spend your money?
How did you meet your spouse?
What made you decide to marry him/her?
What events most changed your life?
Was higher education important to you?
If so, what educational experiences were pivotal in your life?
How did you decide what to study?
How did you choose your vocation and how have you liked it?
How many jobs have you had and which did you like most? Least?

Who to Interview:

On Chart #3, write the names of anyone and everyone in your family that you know. Pulling out your old Christmas card lists or wedding register may help. Once you have generated a list of about twenty or more relatives, look over the list. Some of the relatives may live far away, or you may not feel close enough to them to make your initial contact a one-on-one interview. Cross these individuals off Chart #3 and write their names on Chart #4 labeled "Written Correspondence Log." Set Chart #4 aside. Now take a look at the rest of the names on Chart #3.

Is there one individual that strikes you as possibly being a gatekeeper? Is there an individual that has outlived all of the other members of his or her immediate family? Is there someone who enjoys telling stories and has a knack for details? After asking yourself these questions, formulate a schedule indicating which person you will contact first.

Before starting an interview, make sure you are prepared with the questions you want to ask. Explain to the individual with whom you are speaking what the purpose of the interview is. Careful notations on your part is essential. It is best to use something to help you catch all of the details, such as a tape recorder or video camera.

Once you have completed an interview, take the time to sit down and look through your notes. Highlight with a marker the key points and any names, dates, or events that may have been mentioned. Take all of the information gathered and input it into the *Ancestry Family Tree* software making your source information the name of the person with whom you had the interview as well as the date and place.

After you exhaust your possibilities from Chart #3 it's time to return to Chart #4 that you set aside. These are the people you will contact through letter writing. It is important to keep a log that records who you have written to and when. When you receive any correspondence back from them, that should be noted on this log as well. An extra copy of the "Written Correspondence Log" can be found in the back of this guide.

Chart #3 –Living Source List

1. _____

2. _____

3. _____

4. _____

5. _____

6. _____

7. _____

8. _____

9. _____

10. _____

11. _____

12. _____

13. _____

14. _____

15. _____

16. _____

17. _____

18. _____

19. _____

20. _____

Chart #4 – Correspondence Record

Ancestry.com

1-2-3 Family Tree

Family _____

Researcher _____

Date Sent	Addressee/Address	Purpose	Date Replied	Results

Form # F105

Letter Writing

Letter writing is still an integral part of the data gathering process. The person receiving the letter has time to consider your questions and to respond. An added bonus, however, is if you happen to have the e-mail address of the person you want to contact. E-mail is quicker and less expensive. In either case, there is no guarantee that the person you write will respond, but if you follow the guidelines listed below, you will increase the likelihood of getting a response.

1. Be courteous. Any letter that could be considered curt, rude, or demanding is certain to be thrown into the trash.

2. Be inclusive. Take the time to identify yourself and to explain your project and the reasons for requesting information.

3. Be specific. Make your questions to the point and do not ask for too much information at one time. Focus on the Five Ws.

4. Be thoughtful. Include a self-addressed, stamped envelope with you request.

5. Be thorough. Keep a letter-writing log in which you note the recipients name, the date the letter was sent, and the date a response was received.

6. Be prompt. When you receive a reply, answer immediately with a thank you note or follow-up letter.

Letter writing will always be an important aspect of gathering genealogical information. Probably the best advice is to put yourself in the position of the individual receiving the request. What information would you need in a letter to process a request?

Querying

A very helpful method of gathering genealogical information is called querying. This method has become more useful with Internet connections and online information. Querying means to post a request for information about an individual in your family tree. In your request, try and be brief and specific. Post your query on a genealogical related bulletin board. Several companies and genealogical societies maintain bulletin boards for this purpose. To query on the Ancestry.com message boards, first type <www.ancestry.com> into your Web browser. Once you are at the Ancestry.com home page, click the menu option "Share" and go to the option "Message Boards." Scroll down until you see the option at the bottom right that reads "Message Board Helps." Under this section you should find all of the information necessary to post and search queries.

Primary Sources

A primary source is a record of an event written, spoken, or photographed by an eyewitness to that event at or near the time the event occurred. Some examples are:

Letters

Eyewitness newspaper accounts

Ship passenger lists

Diaries

Deeds and other land ownership records

Baptismal certificates

Photographs of family reunions

Business ledgers with notes in the margins

Military records

Family Bibles that list births, marriages, or family events

Census records

Home videos

Voice recordings, oral histories

Immigration records

Wills

Regroup and Move On

You have just completed STEP ONE. Your family tree should be looking fuller now than it did when you were just writing down the Five Ws about yourself. Depending on how much research others in your family have done, you may be well on your way to knowing many of your ancestors. But there is still work to be done.

STEPS TWO and THREE take you further into your investigation. STEP TWO will teach you how to research your family tree using your computer, the Internet and genealogical databases. STEP THREE will show you how to continue that research using other non-Internet related methods. Both STEPS TWO and THREE involve searching *primary and secondary sources. A primary source* is the most fundamental of all written records. It is a record of an event by an eyewitness to that event at or near the time the event occurred. *A secondary source* is a written record of an event created some time after the event occurred. Usually they are transcriptions of the original records or the compilation of information taken from a variety of sources.

Secondary Sources

Secondary sources are written records of events created some time after the event occurred. Usually they are copies of the original records or the compilation of information taken from a variety of sources. Some examples are:

Family Histories
Town and County Histories
Genealogical Dictionaries
Family Association Newsletters
Genealogical Society Newsletters
Historical Society Publications
Ethnic Society Publications
Newspaper Obituaries
Published Cemetery Inscriptions
Biographies
College Yearbooks

STEP TWO
Researching Your Tree Online

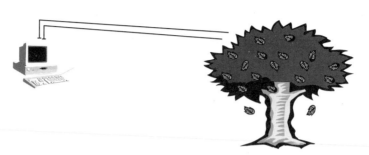

IN STEP TWO YOU WILL:

- Become familiar with the genealogical Web site Ancestry.com

- Conduct a global search in thousands of databases

- Learn how to limit or increase database matches by defining parameters

- Access the Ancestry.com Web site through Ancestry Family Tree software

- Merge pertinent pedigree files from the Ancestry World Tree database

- Extend the branches of your family tree

By now you have gathered enough information to realize that you can't research everyone at once. This is the time to make a choice. Ask yourself, "Which family line do I want to pursue?" Once you decide which family line you want to continue investigating, choose a key individual who is your main point of interest. Choosing this person may entail closing your eyes and pointing at the pedigree chart, or you may feel driven to search out a certain family line. How you choose your key individual is up to you. What matters is that you are now ready for your next line of attack.

Up until this point you have used sources of information that were familiar to you. To go any further you may have to leave your comfort zone and learn to use more complex sources of information. This is the nitty-gritty of family history, and it can be just as fun as looking through old boxes in the attic.

Chart #5 –Research Calendar

Family _____   Researcher _____

Date	Repository Call # Microfilm #	Description of Source	Time Period/ Names Searched	Results

Form # F102

Now that you have decided which key individual you want to make the focus of your search, fill in his or her name in the appropriate space on Chart #5. This research log will help you keep track of what research avenues you have and haven't pursued for a particular person. Not keeping a research log is the one way to waste your time in family history.

On to the Search

There are two ways to begin. You can choose either. The first method is to go directly to the Ancestry.com Web site and do a global search from the home page. The second way is to pull up your pedigree chart in *Ancestry Family Tree* and click on the key individual's name on the pedigree. This will automatically start a global search in the databases at Ancestry.com through your Web browser. If you receive a message saying the program could not find your Web browser, you may have to manually open it. It depends on how your computer and Internet service is set up.

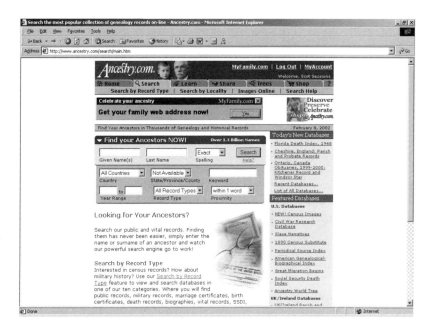

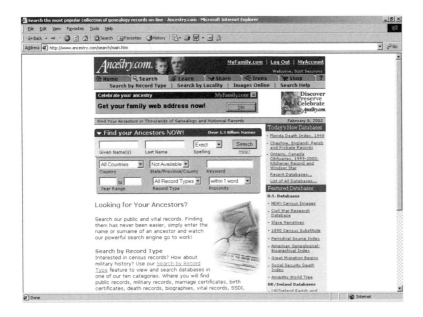

Searching Directly on the Web Site

Let's begin with the first method of doing a global search. A global search means to do a general search of all the databases available. On Ancestry.com's home page there are empty fields where it asks you for given name(s) and surname. It also asks for country; state, province, county; year; and year range. For your first search, only fill in the given name(s) and surname fields. Click on the search button.

Your search results will appear. There are three possible scenarios:

1. Your search yielded no matches.

2. Your search yielded too many matches.

3. Your search yielded a fair amount of matches.

Use the following instructions depending upon what your search results yielded.

Scenario 1:

If your search yielded no matches, then you must try to generalize the search even more. Start eliminating specific parameters. First of all, delete the middle name from the "Given name(s)" field. Click on the "Search" button again.

Even though you may feel absolutely sure that you have correctly spelled the name, try using the Soundex. (See Soundex Instructions below.) This broadens your search. After changing the name to fit within the Soundex parameters, click on the "Search" button.

If you still have no luck, the next option is to try searching by record using a wildcard search. To do this, go to the menu item "Search" and click the option "Search by Record Type." This will give you a listing of all of the major categories of databases available. Click "Birth, Marriage & Death Records." Scroll down and put a wildcard in the "Given" or "Last Name" field. For a wildcard search, use an asterisk.

Using the Soundex

Prior to the enactment of Social Security in the 1930s, Congress needed to know how many people might potentially qualify for benefits under the new, national relief scheme. The census, particularly from 1880, seemed to offer the most reliable estimate of how many recipients there might be. However, no adequate index existed for the 1880 census, and the sheer numbers of Americans counted in 1880 made any indexing a daunting task.

The National Archives recommended using a different indexing system. This became the Soundex system. The Works Progress Administration hired individuals to go through the census data beginning with the 1880 census and create a Soundex card—an actual 3x5 card—for each main entry in the census. In 1880, only families with children age ten and under were included in the Soundex.

In the Soundex scheme, all surnames are reduced to a four-character code and a uniform set of rules applied to the process. A simplified list of rules follows:

1. Print out the name you wish to code. Example: WILLARD

2. Keep the first letter but remove all remaining vowels and the letters H, W, and Y. Example: WILLARD would become WLLRD (the I and A are dropped)

3. Keep the first letter but remove one consonant from any double (back to back) consonants. Example: WLLRD would be reduced to WLRD

4. Keep the first letter and use the Coding Guide to assign the appropriate number to the next three remaining consonants.

For example, if you are searching for a person that you think has the name George Putnam, try putting an asterisk in the given name field or perhaps a "G*" and then put a "P*" in the surname field. Then choose a locality or state in which you think the person may have been born, married, or died. Click the "Search" button.

If you still yield no results, or if none of the matches are the key individual for whom you are looking, then go back to the "Birth, Marriage & Death Records" page. Click on the line that reads "See the FAQs for Birth, Marriage & Death Records." Read through the information to see if the key individual for whom you are looking falls into a time period or category where there are no Birth, Marriage & Death Records (at least not online).

Try a wildcard search by also using the census records found under the "Search" menu option and "Search by Record Type." You may want to do a general locality search by going to the menu item "Search" and then clicking onto the item "Search by Locality." Click onto the state you feel your ancestor may have lived in most of his or her life. Then, put some sort of wildcard again into the name field.

Coding Guide

B, F, P, V 1
C, G, J, K, Q, S, X, Z 2
D, T 3
L 4
M, N 5
R 6

Remember, the vowels (A, E, I, O, U) and the letters H, W, and Y are not considered at all. WILLARD is reduced to WLRD so the Soundex code is W463.
To use another example, JONES would be reduced to JNS. This would convert to J520. Note that if less than three characters follow the first letter, zeroes are used as place fillers. The name LEE would be reduced to just L and the Soundex code would thus be L000. As a final example, HENDERSHOT would be reduced to HNDRST and the Soundex code would be H536. Note that the code stops after the fourth character, even if there are consonants remaining.

Now try your own name in the spaces below:

Your Name: __ __ __ __ __ __ __ __ __ __ __ __ __ __ __

Soundex: __ __ __ __ __ __ __ __ __ __ __ __ __ __ __

When doing a wildcard search, the main idea is to limit the number of databases before putting an asterisk into one of the name fields. Otherwise, a wildcard search will yield too many records to make it worthwhile your time to look through. You can use a wildcard search to look through any of the types of records you feel may be important to your search. Just be sure to try and use any limiting parameters you may know to simplify the search.

To find a listing of all of the databases available at Ancestry.com, go to the home page and scroll down to the lower right hand corner. There you will find a link that shows a complete listing of all the databases online.

Other Useful References in Ancestry.com

The Ancestry Library is a collection of family history how-to and learning materials on the Internet. It is easy to use because of its keyword search feature. In the library you can browse archives of *Ancestry* Magazine, the *Ancestry Daily News*, and popular Ancestry.com online columnists. Every day additional items are added to the Library.

If you have had no luck, don't be discouraged. First of all, record all of your failed attempts on the "Key Individual Research Log." This is important information! You haven't given up on the person, but you may have to try other research methods that are covered in STEP THREE. However, before you stop your online search for that person, there is one more thing you may want to do if you haven't already. Try querying using the Ancestry.com message boards.

To query using the message boards, click the menu item "Share" and click on the item "Message Boards." Scroll down until you see the option at the bottom right that reads "Message Board Helps." Under this section you should find all of the information necessary to post a query and search other queries. Check the site periodically to see if anyone has responded to your query.

Keep in mind that the Ancestry.com databases are continually growing. What is not there today, may appear in a few months time. Try looking for information about this individual again about every six to eight months.

Scenario 2:

In the second scenario, the original global search yielded too many matches. What you can do is add more parameters to your search. For example, add a middle initial or name in the "Given Name(s)" field. Try indicating a place in the "Country" or "State, Province, County" fields. If you have a year, type it in the "Year" field. If you don't have a specific year but can guess as to the time this person was alive, then type that guess in the "Year Range" field. Just add one new parameter at a time and then retry the search.

You can also create more parameters to your search by going under the menu item "Search" and selecting either "Search by Record Type" or "Search by Locality." If you are searching by record type, choose a main database such as Census records or Birth, Marriage, & Death records. A locality is usually defined by state if in the United States or by country if outside the United States. Once you have tried adding more parameters to your search, you should have results that are much more manageable to look through. Now go to Scenario 3.

Special Database in Ancestry.com Ancestry World Tree

Ancestry World Tree is the largest database of family tree files available online. Through World Tree you can access more than 150 million names. Finding leads and collaborating with other genealogists has never been easier. If you find information in the Ancestry World Tree database, you can confirm whether that information is accurate by contacting the contributor and asking for documentation. Ancestry World Tree has been available since 1997.

Everyone benefits from sharing research and collaborating with others. When you submit your family tree you help the Ancestry World Tree grow. If you decide to upload your pedigree information onto Ancestry.com's World tree, as a note of caution be sure to eliminate from your pedigree all living persons.

Scenario 3:

In Scenario 3, your search yielded a reasonable number of matches to look through. Start by clicking open the different databases wherein the matches were found. See if any of the matches could be your key individual by cross referencing the match with other information you may know such as where or when you believe this person was born, lived, or died, etc. Once you

> A good way to not become confused with all of the different sheets of information you may print out is to reference them using the Reference Individual Number (RIN) that *Ancestry Family Tree* assigns each person in your pedigree chart. Write this number on all information related to that person.

determine that a possible match is a definite match, either copy down the information on the "Key Individual Research Log" or print the screen. Attach your printout to your "Key Individual Research Log."

The match or matches you have found are usually secondary sources that have been gathered from original sources. Depending upon which record is found, these secondary sources have a lot of important information about the person such as his or her age, birthplace, birthdate, spouse name, death date, etc.

If you want to view the primary document from which the secondary source was made, there are several things you can do. First, check to see if the match you are viewing has an icon in the upper right hand corner that says "View Image Online." If there is such an icon, this means that the primary source is available online. Click on the image icon. (You may be required to download a viewer or plug in. The download is free, easy to do, and has step-by-step instructions.)

If no image is available, then scroll down on the match screen until you see the link "More Information about this Database." Click and you will receive in-depth information about the primary record from which this information was taken. Using the reference information from the secondary source match, you can locate either the actual primary source or a microfilm on which the original document is recorded. The way to do this is discussed in STEP THREE.

Searching Ancestry.com through Ancestry Family Tree

The second method to begin a global search is to go into the Pedigree page in *Ancestry Family Tree.* Click on the key individual's name you are researching. This will automatically start a global search in the databases at Ancestry.com. If the program indicates that it can't find your Web browser, you may have to manually open it.

In the pedigree chart you will see two numbers on the right side of the name field. They are set apart by asterisks and the words "trees" and "records." The numbers next to the asterisks indicate the number of matches found. Click on either the number of trees (electronic pedigree files submitted by others that may contain the name you have indicated) or the number of records (possible matches of the individual's name in the databases).

This will take you to the Ancestry.com site where you can now search in the matches for your actual key individual.

Charts and Forms

In Ancestry.com under the menu items "Trees" is the option "Charts and Forms." On this page, you can download for free the following useful charts:

Ancestral Chart—Allows you to record the ancestors from whom you directly descend.

Research Calendar—Gives an account of every record source you have searched.

Research Extract—Summarizes information that may be time-consuming or difficult to reread quickly.

Census Extraction—Allows you to record census information. Forms are available for each decennial census from 1790 to 1930.

Correspondence Record—Helps you keep track of those with whom you have corresponded.

Family Group Sheet—Enables you to record complete family information.

Source Summary—Provides quick reference to information and sources you have found for a particular family.

The same three scenarios discussed in the first method are possible in the second method. You may find that the individual's name brought up no matches, too many matches, or a reasonable number of matches to view. Follow the instructions in the previous method according to the different scenarios.

Recording Your Results

Be sure to record all of the results from online searches about your key individual. If you have found matches in the databases from official sources, print the screen and attach it to the "Key Individual Research Log."

If you have found matches in the Ancestry World Tree database (which is a collection of donated pedigree charts from other Ancestry.com users) then you have the capacity to merge that information into your existing pedigree, thus eliminating the need to recopy it.

To merge the tree information, first go to your pedigree chart in *Ancestry Family Tree*. Click on the number of tree matches found (at the upper right corner of a name field.) Scroll through the matches until you find the correct one. Click on the individual's name or the pedigree icon under the name. This will bring up another page that has the option listed near the top to "Merge with *Ancestry Family Tree*." Click on this link. This will bring up another screen that asks if you want to merge the entire pedigree or selective parts. Choose what information from the pedigree on Ancestry.com you want placed into your pedigree in *Ancestry Family Tree*. After the file is imported, you will be prompted to merge the imported tree with your existing tree. You can use the browse button to find and select the two individual entries you want merged. In the left field, indicate the original individual in your *Ancestry Family Tree*. In the right field, indicate the duplicate match from the imported file. Click on the "Merge" button, then click on the close button. While extremely helpful, the information you download from the Ancestry World Tree database needs to be checked for accuracy and reliability.

Repeating the Process

Once you feel you have exhausted the online databases for one individual, choose another name from your family tree that needs researching and start over. Make each individual his or her own "Key Individual Research Log," and then gather information on each person, one-by-one. When you do decide to go to a library or genealogical research center to look for primary sources or to search other secondary sources, your trip will be more productive if you have done as much online searching as you can.

STEP THREE
The Search Continues

IN STEP THREE YOU WILL:

- Learn about general genealogical resources such as: vital records, census records, and the SSDI

- Understand how to use specialized genealogical resources such as: immigration and naturalization papers, military records, land records, wills and probates, and court records

- Learn the steps of writing letters to government offices

- Make a successful trip to a library or genealogical center

- Fill in the branches to your family tree

Congratulations! Now that you have reached STEP THREE, your family tree is most likely looking very healthy. Reaching STEP THREE means you should no longer call yourself a beginning genealogist. You are moving on to intermediate methods of research.

In STEP ONE you created the foundation to your family tree. In STEP TWO you tapped into the high-tech resources of the Internet to give your tree more branches. In STEP THREE you will learn how to make sure those branches are laden and flourishing with information. It really is a step-by-step process. This 1-2-3 formula for researching your family tree is illustrated by the story of Ellen, a mother who started her genealogy during the hours her children were at school.

Italy Discovered

Ellen became interested in connecting with her lost Italian heritage when her youngest child entered first grade and she suddenly had some free time.

During this time she turned to the Internet and found that she needed a few solid facts to begin her research. She called her mom, asked where her family had come from, and was given the name of a little town in Sicily.

Her mother had ample information about the three generations of their family since they had come to America in the early 1900s. However, she knew little about why the family had left Italy or exactly when they came.

Armed only with the names of her grandparents and the name of her ancestral home, Ellen discovered a Web site called RootsWeb.com that had an e-mail mailing list specifically for people researching ancestors from Sicily. From it, she learned about all kinds of resources, including a genealogy center right in her hometown.

From the center, she gained access to the 1920 Federal Census. Much to her delight she found her great-grandparents listed with all their children, including her grandma, who was only a baby at the time. The census gave her several clues that helped her in her search.

Next she sent a request to the National Archives for passenger lists. They sent her documents showing the name of the ship her family had traveled on and their date of processing through Ellis Island when they arrived here. She located first-hand accounts of what it was like to travel by ship in those days and to be processed into the country through Ellis Island.

On the Internet she also found an information request form letter written in Italian. She filled in known family facts and sent the form to the civil records office in Sicily. Several weeks later she received a printout containing birth dates, marriage dates, and immigration dates for her great-grandmother's family. The facts she gathered eventually led her to contact living relatives in Sicily, whom she recruited to help in her investigative efforts. She eventually ended up with enough information to write a family history that tied generations together and created a closer bonding with her living family.

Finding Useful Sources

Like Ellen, once you have researched information on several key individuals using the Internet, you may have found the need to try and locate a primary record. While some primary sources are available online, many are not. You may need to search at libraries, government offices, and genealogical centers for records not yet available through Internet sources.

In STEP THREE you will learn information about some of the more common records used in genealogy. You will learn ways to find primary source information, as well as ways to find sources of secondary information. Before spending time in a library trying to find certain information, be sure you are not redoing work that you already did online. For example, if you decide a certain land record may prove useful, go online to Ancestry.com and check to make sure you have not already searched that record in a global search. To find the names of the databases available at Ancestry.com, go to the home page and scroll down to the lower right hand corner. There you will find a link that shows a complete listing of all the sources online.

Read through all of STEP THREE at least once. This will give you an idea of what research options are available. Then, look at the key individual you are researching and ask yourself these questions relating to him/her:

1. Is it possible that his or her vital records could be available through another source? (Remember, before pursuing a library research project make sure the index you are going to look for isn't already online at Ancestry.com.)

2. How could census records of relatives of this individual help me locate him/her? (e.g., A census record could give you a location of the key individual's children, and that could lead you to some sort of a land record.)

3. Are passenger lists or naturalization records pertinent to him/her?

4. Was he or she possibly in the military? If yes, what time period and during which wars?

5. Would land records be available since I know a location of his/her main residency?

6. Do I know his or her death date and location to look up a will or probate that may give me little known facts about this person?

7. Do I know enough about him or her to make court records a possible link to more in-depth information?

Decide what your next step is based upon your answers to these questions. Once you have narrowed down what type of record may be of use to you, read carefully again through the related section in STEP THREE. Try to learn as much as you can about the types of records you will be researching. More reference information is available through the "Library" or "Shop" menu options found on the home page of Ancestry.com.

Vital Records

Vital records are records of life events important enough that some level of government acquires, organizes, and preserves them. In genealogy, the term vital record refers specifically to birth, marriage, and death events. As a general rule, these records are maintained by the level of government closest to where the event actually took place. In most of the United States the city, town, or county government maintains the records. Since the end of the nineteenth century, each state also records each of these events. These are maintained at the state's capital by an office of vital records, vital statistics, etc. A good guideline to keep in mind is: If the event occurred before 1900, the local community would be the best place to seek the vital record; if the event occurred after 1900, either the local or state level would be a good place to start.

Birth Records

Most birth records, especially earlier ones, contain only basic information. In an early New England birth record, for example, you are likely to find the name of the child, date and place of birth, and parents' names. By the mid-nineteenth century, birth records became a little more informative.

Writing to Request Vital Records

When writing to a local, county (parish), state, or national office to request some type of vital record (birth, marriage, divorce, death, etc.), the following guidelines will make the task easier and more productive:

1. Determine the correct address of the office and department you wish to contact to avoid having your letter buried in a dead letter file somewhere. You can also go online to locate information on addresses, costs, and even the electronic availability of records for numerous jurisdictions throughout the United States and the world.

2. Determine the correct fee the office charges for the service you are requesting. The same sources used to provide the address should provide the cost for various records. Always enclose a check or money order for the exact amount; never send cash. NARA payment information is included on the form.

3. Finally, provide specific information for each person you are seeking records about. This information should include:

    a. the specific record you want

    b. full name of the person whose record is being requested

    c. sex and race

    d. parents' names in full with mother's maiden name

    e. day, month, and year of known events in the person's life

    f. full place name where known events occurred (town, county, state)

    g. reason you are requesting the record

    h. your relationship to the person whose record is being requested.

Marriage Records

Ironically, in some states the government required marriage records to be kept before birth and death records were required. This stems from the legal implications of the ownership of property in a marriage. There are two types of marriage records: first, the marriage application and, second, the proof of marriage. In a marriage application record you may find information such as the names of the bride and groom, their residence, race, age, dates and places of birth, previous marriages, occupations, and their parents' names.

Death Records

Much like the birth records, early death records are simple records that typically give the name of the deceased, the date of death, and the place of death. Obituary records and cemetery records are more likely to give you more information, but these records are not always as easily found as death records.

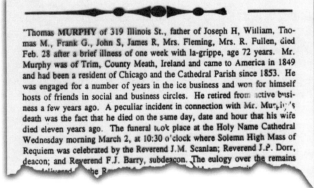

It is rare for the researcher to be able to view death records personally. Instead, a records request form must be completed, either at the appropriate office or by mail. After doing so, and as long as the necessary information is supplied, you will receive a copy of the record(s) requested. As you might expect, there are fees for these copies.

Another way in which to view a vital record is through the use of microfilm. Many vital records have been compiled onto microfilm. Some private genealogy centers and public libraries have access to these microfilms.

Use a phone book or an Internet phone number/address database to locate any libraries and genealogical centers near you. The obvious problem in conducting vital records research is knowing where to go or where to write for the information. These are some prominent sources that may help: *Ancestry's Redbook: American State, County and Town Sources* edited by Alice Eichholz, Ph.D., C.G.; and *The Source: A Guidebook of American Genealogy* edited by Loretto Dennis Szucs and Sandra Hargreaves Luebking.

Census Records

A census is a complete count of a population. In the United States, both federal and state governments have been conducting censuses in one form or another since the eighteenth century.

Although census records were never intended to be genealogical records, they have become a boon to genealogists. Use federal census records as a starting point. Your online search hopefully yielded some census information about some of your ancestors.

The good thing about census research is that the federal census records—especially those since 1850—are readily available, except for the 1890 Federal Census records, which were destroyed in a fire. The 1890 substitute records at Ancestry.com are a compilation of other records from that time period.

The first U.S. federal population census was conducted in 1790, and a population census has been conducted every ten years since then. Due to federal privacy laws, no federal records within a seventy-two year period are open to the public. Thus, the 1930 census, released in April 2002, is the most recent federal census available to researchers. One of the rules of sound genealogical research is to start with yourself and work backward in time, moving from the known to the unknown. So start with the most recent census available.

40

SSDI (Social Security Death Index)

In 1935, Franklin D. Roosevelt signed the Social Security Act into law. Since that time the government has issued more than 400 million social security numbers. The Social Security Administration has indexed the deaths of 60 million of those 400 million people into one of the largest databases available (SSDI). As these numbers show, not everyone who was issued a Social Security number is in the SSDI. However, the SSDI is a great source to track down information about family members within the last four decades. About 98 percent of the SSDI records represent individuals who have died after 1962.

The SSDI is an extremely valuable source to help an adopted child find birth parents or to help someone who has lost contact with his or her family to find them. The SSDI can also be a stepping stone to other records such as obituaries, cemetery records, and official death records. If you are able to locate the exact date and place of death from the SSDI, then more records are opened up to further your investigation.

The SSDI is available for you to search online at Ancestry.com. When you perform a search you will be returned with any matches in the database. In the upper right hand corner of an SSDI match record, there is the option to "Request Information." If you click on this link, it takes you to a page called, "Writing a Letter to the Social Security Administration." From this page you can automatically generate a letter that has all the pertinent information on the individual you are researching.

Immigration Records and Passenger Lists

Virtually every American can trace his or her family history back to an ancestor who entered this country as an immigrant. Estimates place the total number of immigrants to this country (1607 to the present) between 35 and 50 million.

Immigration records are divided into two time periods. From the earliest Colonial period until approximately 1820 immigration records were kept by the colony or state where the port was located. The federal government did not require ship captains to present a list to port authorities. The immigration records that exist may be found in either the port city or in the archives for that state and are usually located in the state's capital. Two excellent general references that detail these records are: *A Bibliography of Ship Passenger Lists, 1583-1825* by Harold Lancour; and *They Came in Ships* by John P. Colletta.

Beginning in 1934, the federal government has kept immigration records in the National Archives in Washington, D.C. Copies of some of these records are also located in the regional branches of the National Archives.

Two types of federal immigration records are:

- Customs passenger lists—These lists were kept by the U.S. Customs Service and cover the years from 1820 until approximately 1891.

- Immigration passenger lists—These lists were kept by the United States Immigration and Naturalization Service (INS). They begin in 1906 and continue until 1957.

Since the vast majority of people entered this country after 1820, the obvious problem is locating information on the one person being traced. Some of the passenger lists have been indexed and are available on microfilm through the National Archives and in major research libraries. Ellis Island is also a great starting point in trying to track down records about your ancestor who immigrated to the United States.

Another way to possibly track immigration information is to start looking in the 1920 Census. Column 13 of the 1920 Census asks for the year of immigration to the United States. This information, while not always accurate, yields a possible key piece of data to pursue. Then, coupled with an educated guess as to the port of entry, you are ready to consult the various indexes available from the National Archives. The NARA Web site gives detailed information on how to request information.

Naturalization Records

When immigrants enter the United States, they are classified as aliens. If they choose, aliens can become citizens. By definition, naturalization is the process by which an alien achieves the status of citizenship and there are documents that accompany this process.

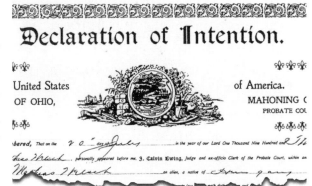

Prior to the American Revolution, citizenship was not a major issue. After 1790, the process of becoming a citizen became more important and was taken over by the new federal government. Congress established a three-step citizenship process that remains in place today.

Step 1: After residing in the United States for at least two years, an alien can declare his or her intent to become a citizen. The paperwork necessary for this first step is known as the Declaration of Intention, or the "petition papers."

Step 2: The alien is required to reside in the United States for a specified period of time, usually an additional three years after the Declaration of Intention is filed.

Step 3: The alien, upon satisfying the first two steps, and after being a resident for at least five years, can petition a court for admission as a citizen. This process is referred to as the "second papers." The court to which this petition is submitted does not have to be the same court to which the first papers were submitted.

If the applicant's papers are deemed to be in order, a Naturalization Certificate, or "third paper," is issued. This is the legal proof of citizenship and often becomes an immigrant's prized possession.

Locating Naturalization Records

Of all the public records available to genealogists, naturalization records are perhaps the most difficult to use because they are so hard to track down. Since immigrant ancestors could begin the process of naturalization at any authorized court, and since virtually any court was authorized, the actual records of naturalization could be scattered over the various levels of American courts—from local and county to state and federal. Fortunately, some of the more recent censuses also asked when an individual was naturalized.

Armed with the knowledge of when the ancestor was naturalized and where that individual might have been residing at the time, the researcher can begin the quest for the court where the papers would have been filed. The best rule of thumb is to begin with the court located nearest the immigrant ancestor's home. For an excellent resource on the levels and locations of various courts around the United States, see *They Became Americans: Finding Naturalization Records and Ethnic Origins* by Loretto Dennis Szucs.

U.S. Census Naturalization Information

Below is a list of some of the more useful census years and the column for that census that might help your search:

1870 Census. Note the column, "Male Citizens of the United States of twenty-one years of age and upwards." If your male ancestor was enumerated in this census and a check appears in column 19, you have a clue that the naturalization occurred before 1870. While that does not pin down the exact year of naturalization, you can use it as a starting point. For example, you might know (from a different source) that your immigrant arrived in 1858, and thus you will have a range of dates to search. Knowing that he must have resided in this country at least two years before filing "petition papers," then the range of possible dates would be between 1860 and 1870.

1900 Census. The 1900 Census requested the individual's naturalization status in column 18. The responses are "AL" for alien, "PA" for having filed petition papers, and "NA" for naturalized. Again, no actual year is provided, but you can use your powers of deductive reasoning to narrow down the possibilities.

1910 Census. The 1910 Census requested the naturalization status in column 16, and the responses are the same as on the 1900 Census.

1920 Census. The 1920 Census records the same data in column 14, but also asks for the exact year in which the individual was naturalized in column 15. Remember that the individual being interviewed was working from memory and that the answer in column 15 may be off by a few years.

After locating the court, write and request a copy of the naturalization papers or personally go to the courthouse. In either case, you must have as much specific information as possible about the ancestor—full name, date of birth, etc. In some cases, naturalization records have been moved to another location, such as a state historical society or even the National Archives. Some naturalization records are online. Go under the "Search" menu item at Ancestry.com and click on to "Search by Record Type." There you will find a list of all naturalization records available. Another good Web site to try is <www.cyndislist.com>.

Military Records

Seventy-five percent of Americans claim that at least one family member has served in the United States' military. Various types of records were created for every individual who served in the United States military. The real concern is learning what and where these records are, and how to use them as a research aid.

The basic steps of learning about your military ancestor are:

1. Identify the individual (full legal name).

2. Identify the military branch.

3. Identify the time period.

4. Identify where the records are kept for that time period.

5. Secure the proper request form.

6. Complete and submit the form.

Military Photos

Consider the clues you can uncover from studying a military photograph in your family photo collection:

1. The picture should identify the individual. Be certain you know the individual's real name. For example, if you knew the soldier as Uncle Frank, his legal name may be Francis or even William Frank. His military records will list him under his legal name.

2. The picture should help you determine the war in which the individual served. Look for clues such as the style of uniform, the clothing style of others in the picture, or objects that can determine a time period, such as an automobile. This information is extremely important, as military records are filed according to the time period served.

3. The photograph should help you identify the branch in which your relative served through the uniform worn. In most cases, military records were kept by branch—army, navy, etc.

4. A careful inspection of the picture may reveal other important clues, such as a symbol or a patch that represents rank or unit (battalion, division, or platoon). Such information is helpful when researching military records.

Breakdown of Location of Military Records

The tables included below detail exactly which records are available and where they can be found.

National Archives and Records Administration: Military Service Records

Service Branch	Rank	Dates of Service
Volunteers	1775-1902	
Army	Officers	1789-June 1917
	Enlisted	1789-31 Oct. 1912
Navy	Officers	1798-1902
	Enlisted	1798-1885
Marine Corps	Officers	1789-1895
	Enlisted	1789-1895
Coast Guard	1791-1919*	
Confederate States		1861-65
Pension files (all claims)	1775-1916	

*Including service to earlier versions of coast guard

    1.   The National Archives does not do research for an individual. When the proper information is supplied, the Archives will provide photocopies of records for a fee.

    2.   To obtain these photocopies, submit standard NATF Form 80, on which you identify the records you seek. Form 80 can be obtained from:

General Reference Branch (NNRG)
National Archives and Records Administration
8th and Pennsylvania Avenue, NW
Washington, DC 20408

National Personnel Records Center (NPRC): Military Personnel Records

Service Branch	Rank	Earliest Service Dates
Air Force	Officers	25 Sept. 1947
	Enlisted	25 Sept. 1947
Army	Officers	Separated 1 Jul. 1917
	Enlisted	Separated 12 Nov. 1912
Navy	Officers	Separated 1 Jan. 1903
	Enlisted	Separated 1 Jan. 1886
Marine Corps	Officers	Separated 1 Jan. 1905
	Enlisted	Separated 1 Jan. 1905
Coast Guard	Officers	Separated 1 Jan. 1898
	Enlisted	Separated 1 Jan. 1898

These records may only be obtained by the individual, a legal representative of the individual, or a family member with written permission of the individual. If the individual has passed away, a family member can obtain the records by proving relationship to the deceased.

Between 16 million and 18 million Army and Air Force records held in St. Louis were destroyed by fire in 1973. Alternate sources can be used to reconstruct any destroyed records, but the reconstruction may not be as complete as the original.

To obtain a copy of any records that do exist, the individual or legal representative must submit Standard Form 180, Request Pertaining to Military Records, for non-genealogical requests, and OR NA Form 13043 for genealogical requests. This form is available from the National Personnel Records Center (Military Personnel Records) at 9700 Page Boulevard, St. Louis, MO, 63132.

Time Period and War

As with other branches of the federal government, the United States military has kept excellent records of the men and women who have served the country. It is entirely possible for an individual to have served in the military at any time during the nation's history. But it is generally during war times that most people, usually young men between the ages of eighteen and thirty, enlisted or were drafted.

Below is a list of wars and major military actions that the United States has participated in since it became a country.

American War Dates	
Revolutionary War	1775-83
Indian Wars	1780s-1800
War of 1812	1812-15
Mexican War	1846-48
Civil War	1861-65
Spanish-American War	1898
Philippine Insurrection	1899-1902
World War I	1917-18
World War II	1941-45
Korean War	1950-53
Vietnam War	1965-73
Gulf War	1991
War on Terrorism	2001

It is important to identify the branch of military in which your ancestor served. A useful general reference book is *U.S. Military Records* by James C. Neagles.

Types of Records

If your ancestor served in the military, the federal military records you should look into are:

- Draft and conscription records

- Enlistment and service records

- Pension records

- National military cemetery records

Service records and pension records tend to be the most accessible and are recommended as a starting place. As you learn more about your military ancestor, you can pursue other records to fill in the details of his or her service. The useful genealogical data you might learn from service records could include the individual's full name, rank, age, physical description, marital status, occupation, city of birth, and place of residence at enlistment.

From pension records you may learn some or all of the following: the applicant's name, spouse's name (possibly even a wife's maiden name), rank, military unit, length of enlistment, and residence at time of application. In some cases, additional information is also included, such as documented proof of service, discharge papers, and even personal information like date and place of birth, marriage, or death.

If you are not certain whether your military ancestor received a pension, the federal government has published lists of pensioners at different times in history. These lists give the soldier's name, service information, age, death date, and even his or her heirs. Such lists are available for the years 1792-95, 1813, 1817, 1818, 1820, 1823, 1828, 1831, 1835, 1840, 1849, 1857, 1883, and 1899. These lists can be found in the U.S. Congressional Serial Set located in federal repository libraries or in the libraries of most major universities. Also, the federal censuses of 1840, and 1910 list veterans and pensioners.

As a rule of thumb, military records from the twentieth century can be found at the National Personnel Records Center (NPRC) located in St. Louis, Missouri, and military records dated before 1900 can be found in the National Archives in Washington, D.C.

Land Records

Land records have provided genealogists with a way to bypass a dead end family line. Land records are plentiful, accessible, easy to use, informative, and interesting.

First, you must try and determine where your key individual may have owned land (in town, in the county, even in the state). If you are uncertain where your ancestor lived, use census records to determine the information. Then determine what types of land records exist for that locality and where you might find them. Most land records in the United States are kept at the county level, with four exceptions. Louisiana's land records are kept at the parish or county level of government, and Connecticut, Rhode Island, and Vermont have land records at the town level.

To try to locate land records, you may need the following information:

1. An accurate date and place.

2. The name of the individual or individuals purchasing the land.

3. Where the family or individual was living when the purchase occurred.

---

3 Benefits of Land Records

1. **Plentiful.** In 1850, 90 percent of free males in the United States owned land, making land records one of the most plentiful sources of genealogical information. Even today, land ownership represents about half of the U.S. population. See E. Wade Hone's book, *Land and Property Research in the United States* (Ancestry, 1997) for more details on land records in the United States.

2. **Accessible.** Every county, parish, or town responsible for keeping land records makes the records available for research. In addition, the Internet is becoming an excellent source of land records. The real beauty of online land records is that they are searchable by name. Easy to Use. In virtually every case, land records are indexed.

3. **Informative.** The data researchers gather from land records can be the breakthrough in the brick wall barrier. Examine who may have owned property adjacent to your ancestors, since adjacent property owners were often somehow related.

Wills and Probate Records

Probate records, or court records created to validate a deceased person's will are useful in the quest for family data for several reasons. First, they relate to information already gathered. If you have gathered death records, you already have two pieces of important information—date and place of death—which make using wills and probate records easier. Next, information gathered from wills is usually reliable. And finally, wills are easy to locate. Very often, there is an index, alphabetical by the name of the testator, for the county in which an ancestor's will was filed for probate. The index will lead to the original document.

To simplify the process of using wills and probate records, follow these basic steps:

1. Identify the Individual

Use the decedent's full name and try to find as much biographical information as possible, including birth, marriage, and family information, in addition to the date of death.

2. Identify the Place of Death

Most wills are filed for probate in the county where the individual was residing at the time he or she passed away. The correct place names for either the city or town and the county are critical for success in locating the will.

Pitfalls of Wills and Probate Records

As with any type of genealogical research, there are certain pitfalls and shortcomings to avoid. Listed below are some of the potential pitfalls in using wills and probate records:

1. Extracts are secondary sources and should not be relied upon.

2. Don't make assumptions based on information in wills, as it can be misleading.

3. Be careful of terms that imply relationships, e.g., sister, cousin, senior, infant. Sister, for example, may refer to a female of the same religious faith or to a sister-in-law, and not to an actual sibling.

4. Wills are not always filed immediately after the individual's death. Search the years following the person's death as well.

5. Witnesses cannot be beneficiaries, but they are often relatives and should be investigated.

6. If a wife is named in a will, do not assume that she is the mother of the named children in the will.

7. Remember that boundaries have changed over time. The researcher must know the correct location to determine the jurisdiction over probate records.

3. Learn Where the Records Are Kept

Wills are usually filed at the county level and can be found in the county court building in the office of probate. However, there are exceptions. To find the exact addresses of these offices, turn to a good reference book like *Ancestry's Red Book*.

4. Learn What Records Are Available

When you're looking for probate records, you might also encounter documents such as inventories, distributions of estates, letters of administration, sales of estates, and inquest documents. Be sure to request all the records that might pertain to the person you are researching, including testate and intestate proceedings. Testate is used to describe a situation when an individual dies with a valid will. Intestate describes the situation when a person dies without leaving a valid will.

5. Access the Records

You may have to request the information by mail. If so, determine the title of the person you will be writing to, the correct mailing address for the person's office, and the cost for the service. As with any written correspondence, be sure to include a SASE for the materials. Also, keep a correspondence log noting the date(s) of your request(s), the amount of money sent, and the date you received any response(s).

6. Analyze and Record the Information

Leave no line unread, especially the part of the will that names the witnesses. Remember to indicate the source of the information.

Court Records

Court records are mainly used to get more extensive information about a person for whom you already have all of the Five Ws. If you think that there may be some court proceedings in that person's life, (e.g., the individual was divorced, etc.) then court records may be a good avenue of research. Listed below are a few of the main court records that may be helpful to pursue:

Adoption

Perhaps the most frustrating brick wall in genealogical research is discovering an adopted ancestor. In most cases, adoption records are sealed. This means that the information is only available to the adoptee when he or she has reached legal age and has secured a court order to access the records. Some courts allow sealed records to be viewed by others when good cause can be proven (such as the need to learn about a genetic medical condition), but this is rare and very difficult to accomplish.

Remember that prior to the twentieth century, it was common for adoptions to be handled quietly, within the family. Thus you may not find a record of the adoption at all.

Divorce

While less common before 1900, divorce is a legal action that has occurred for many years. Divorce papers were filed at the local court level. In some cases, the divorce proceedings were initiated, but never completed. But even in such a case, documents can be found that may contain some useful genealogical information.

Pitfalls and Limitations of Court Records

There are limitations to the value of court records.

First, the indexes (if there are indexes) are not the complete record. They are secondary sources, transcribed by a clerk to serve only one purpose: to lead you to the actual record itself. Also, not all court records have been fully indexed. Should you encounter such a set of records, roll up your sleeves and be prepared for some old-fashioned detective work.

Second, the original source might be difficult to locate. Towns and counties have changed significantly over the decades in terms of the records they keep. How the records are stored in that community is no exception.

Guardianships

While guardianship records may seem unusual, they are more common than you might expect. In many cases, a widow could not always care for her children. If she could not remarry, she may have had to make her children wards of the state. They would most likely be placed in an orphanage, but it is also possible that the court appointed a guardian. Also, guardianship might have been arranged in a man's will (so that his children would be taken care of after his death). In any case, the court would have documentation of the guardianship. Related documents may come from what some regions refer to as Orphan's Court, so be sure to determine what such a court might be called in the area you are researching.

Other Sources

There are, of course, other sources you can use to further your genealogical research. Each type of record lends itself to a lot of details as you have seen in STEP 3. The best way to go about using these other sources is to get a book that covers that type of record. Specific books for many different sources are available under the menu item "Shop" at Ancestry.com. There is also a lot of resource information under the menu item "Library."

A Trip to the Library

Good detectives have their favorite places to go where the locals who know everything "hang out." A genealogist also has a place full of great information—a library.

In STEP TWO you were introduced to online sources from which you can search thousands of databases. In the first part of STEP THREE you were introduced to both the general and specialized records available. If unavailable online, many of these general and specialized records are available at larger libraries.

In addition, at local libraries you can find local histories and archives of local newspapers. Such things are specific to the city or county in which they were originally

Before Leaving Home

Once you have decided which library may be of the most importance to you, check and see if it has a Web site that supplies you with the information you need. If not, call ahead and find out what the days and hours of operation are. You many want to ask some of the following questions:

1. Is there an orientation tour of the library? Do you need to sign up in advance? (Orientation sessions can save hours of valuable time by helping you learn what is available and where to find it. You will also meet a staff member who might be a good contact person to answer questions that may arise later.)

2. Does the library have any special requirements like picture ID or to be a local resident?

3. Is it necessary to sign up in advance to use special equipment such as microfilm readers, microfiche readers, or computers?

4. Is parking available and what does it cost? Some libraries are located in the heart of a city and the only available parking is in a nearby garage that charges.

5. Are laptops allowed in the library? Many researchers bring their laptops with them, but you should check first to find out what the library's policy is on portable computers. If they are allowed, remember to carry all of your valuables with you when you leave your workspace.

printed. However, sources at a local library may not be well indexed and they may be difficult to use. Also, they represent the type of research that requires many hours of work with little or even sometimes no payoff. However, when you do find some piece of relevant information, the payoff in satisfaction seems well worth the time invested. In most cases (except for family histories) you should turn to these local sources only when other sources have produced nothing. Use these sources as a break from your other research. Local printings of family histories are the exception. They are usually easy to use and give lots of information.

If you decide a trip to the local library may be useful, start by making a list of all research centers and libraries near your home. This list should include your local public library, your local historical society, genealogical society, ethnic society, even a nearby college library.

Essential Library Tools

1. **Pencils.** It is always a good idea to use a pencil in all of your preliminary research. Some libraries require researchers to use only pencil.

2. **Reading glasses.** Some of the material that one discovers can be difficult to read even under the best conditions.

3. **Magnifying glass.** Some material is difficult to read even with good light and a good pair of glasses. A magnifying glass or magnifying bar can help.

4. **Blank research forms or a laptop computer.** Once you discover useful material, you need to record this information. Putting the information directly on research forms or into the computer cuts down one step.

5. **Change.** Photocopy machines usually take change or require a photocopy card. Carry some extra cash so you can copy things you find.

When visiting your local library, there are certain "sections" in the library that you should try to locate. Some of these sections are:

1. Local history–If the family you are researching came from the town in which the library is located, this collection will contain information you will turn to frequently.

2. Published family histories—In some communities, it is only at a local library where a family history can be found.

3. Indexes–Some very useful sources (like obituaries) have been indexed and these indexes offer the researcher an excellent starting point.

4. Newspapers–An excellent source of genealogy material comes from local newspapers including obituaries and even published births and marriages. Some local newspapers have even been indexed.

5. Maps and gazetteers—Any research in a particular geographic area requires knowledge of the area. These maps and gazetteers provide that information.

All libraries are different. There are pros and cons to each. Here is an introduction to some of the different kinds of libraries out there.

- **Local public libraries** usually contain varying amounts of information. Usually they have a very strong collection of books, maps, and vital records relating to their own communities. Their reference librarians can also tell you who the local genealogy experts are and how to contact them.

- **Local historical society libraries** have excellent information relating to the community, especially their collections of pictures, artifacts, maps, clothing, and other items of local interest. This unique information adds texture to your research as you learn more about the community (and possibly even the homes) in which your ancestors resided.

- **Local genealogical society libraries** focus on the unique and the old. If your ancestors lived in one area for a long period of time, or were early settlers in that area, there may be unique research available on the families from that town, such as the only copy of research done by a local historian.

- **County public libraries** are maintained when there is a group of small towns that don't have their own libraries. These are excellent places for research as they have information relating to all the towns within their boundary.

- **County historical society libraries** are similar to their local counterparts, except they have information on the entire county. They may also contain displays and dioramas that make the history of their county come alive.

- **State libraries** are usually located in the state's capital city. They can be a valuable source of genealogical information. It may have information that helps if you had ancestors that migrated between towns within a state. In some states, the state archives are located in the same complex as the state library.

- **State historical societies** house materials of interest to both historians and to genealogists. They often contain excellent collections and are located in historic buildings.

- **Regional research libraries** are not very common. However, there are several regional libraries in the United States, and an excellent example is the New England Historic Genealogical Society located in Boston, Massachusetts. This library houses a tremendous collection of materials that relate to New England research. This facility is a necessary visit for those who can trace their roots to New England.

- **Ethnic genealogical society libraries** house materials relating to a particular ethnic group. One particularly noteworthy library is the American-Canadian Genealogical Society (ACGS) Library in Manchester, New Hampshire. This library has an outstanding collection relating to Franco-American, Acadian, and French-Canadian genealogy.

- **National libraries** are huge and take some time to get oriented. Two such libraries are the National Archives located in Washington, D.C., which contains a huge collection of materials relating to all aspects of genealogy. Central to these materials are federal records such as census, military, and public land records. The other national library is the Family History Library located in Salt Lake City, Utah. This library houses the world's leading collection of primary and secondary source material, much of which is available on microforms and on loan for use at its family history centers located throughout the United States.

Published Family Histories

When beginning research at your local library, start with the published family histories. If research has already been done on your family, you may find a great deal of information from which you will benefit. These volumes are usually displayed in alphabetical order by the name of the principal family covered in the book. Also, some libraries have an index of all the families covered in these volumes, in addition to the name or names listed in the title.

These compiled secondary sources often yield a complete history for one line of your research. As with any book, they can take several different formats. To determine if the book contains relevant information, first check the index and see if the name for which you are searching appears. See if the index offers any additional information for each primary entry such as a place name, event, or essential date associated with that person. Once you find pertinent information, be sure to double-check it using other sources. Family histories are not always accurate.

Unfortunately, in some published family histories there is no index. In this case, review the contents of the book by skimming the pages looking for clues associated with the name you are researching. Patience and perseverance can yield results but remember that a book without an index can be one of the most frustrating situations you will encounter in your family history research.

Other Sources

After searching the family histories, if you still have time at the library, turn your attention to local histories. Many have specific family information included in them, and some have genealogies on two or more generations of a particular family.

Next, utilize the collection of local newspapers to search for the names of your ancestors that were from the area. A birth, death, or special event may have been published. A fourth area to consider at a local library, if it is available, is a military sources. Military resources are usually arranged in chronological order, beginning with the earliest conflicts and continuing to the present.

A Hobby with the Ultimate Reward

After nineteen years of searching for information about her grandmother, Jeanne thought it was hopeless. Her grandmother would always remain a mystery. Jeanne's grandparents were divorced when Jeanne's mother was a baby. Then, at six years of age, Jeanne's mother was taken by her father and hidden with relatives in another state. Jeanne's mother never saw her mother again.

Ever since Jeanne started doing genealogy, one of her goals was to find information about her lost grandmother. However, she had not had much luck for nearly twenty years. Then, on a Wednesday morning, Jeanne linked up to Ancestry.com. In minutes, using the Social Security Death Index and just her grandmother's first name and birth date, Jeanne found her. Finally… a record of her grandmother. The SSDI record gave Jeanne her grandmother's married name for her second marriage. Using that name and the location of the grandmother's birth, she was able to contact her lost grandmother's daughter-in-law. A relative Jeanne never knew existed.

Jeanne learned wonderful information from her newly found relatives. She learned that her grandmother had been a nurse, and that she had adopted an abandoned baby boy. And more than anything else, Jeanne felt a connection that she had never known before. For Jeanne, her hobby of genealogy had brought her the ultimate reward.

Finding Those Who Were Lost

As you continue to search out your ancestors, you too may find those who have been lost for centuries, or maybe just a few decades such as was the case with Jeanne. No matter how long the separation, the moment when you rediscover who you are and where you came from is always a moment to cherish. Doing genealogy can be a lifelong interest. The family tree that you created by following the steps in this guide will give enjoyment and a sense of belonging to not only yourself, but to your own descendants for years to come.

Bibliography

Colletta, John P. *They Came in Ships*, SLC, Utah: Ancestry, 1993.

Eichholz, Alice Ph.D., C.G. *Ancestry's Redbook: American State, County and Town Sources*, SLC, Utah: Ancestry, Revised 1992.

Lancour, Harold. *A Bibliography of Ship Passenger Lists*, 1583-1825, New York: New York Public Library, 1978.

Neagles, James, C. U.S. *Military Records*. SLC, Utah: Ancestry, 1994.

Szucs, Loretto Dennis and Luebking, Sandra Hargreaves. *The Source*. SLC, Utah: Ancestry, Revised 1996.

Szucs, Loretto Dennis. *They Became Americans: Finding Naturalization Records and Ethnic Origins*, SLC, Utah: Ancestry, 1998.

Glossary

Census A complete counting of a population.

Customs Passenger Lists Records kept by the U.S. Customs Service of immigrants.

Databases A collection of information organized for rapid search and retrieval with a computer.

Family or Birth Name Last name at birth.

Gatekeeper Usually an older member in an extended family who keeps much of the family knowledge and/or heirlooms.

Genealogical Research Center Either a private or public office where genealogical records are available for research.

Generation A single step in the line of descent from an ancestor.

Given Name A first and middle name.

Global Search A general search of all databases in a collection.

Immigration Passenger Lists Records kept by the U.S. Immigration and Naturalization Service of immigrants.

Land Record A record showing the buyer and seller of a piece of property.

Naturalization Record An official government record showing when and where an alien became a U.S. citizen.

Parameters A boundary or limit in a search. A parameter in a genealogical search could be given or last name, place, year, type of record, etc.

Pedigree Chart A register recording a line of ancestors.

Primary Source A record of an event by an eyewitness to that event at or near the time the event occurred.

Query To ask a question about an ancestor to an unknown audience in order to receive confirmation or new information.

Research Log A written record of research.

Secondary Source A written record of an event created long after the event occurred.

SSDI or Social Security Death Index An index of the death benefits of those persons assigned a social security number.

Surname The last name or family name.

The Five Ws Who, what, when, where, and why.

Vital Records Records of life events preserved by an official source (e.g., government).

Interview Questions

Who:

Were you close to any of your grandparents?
If so, what are your favorite memories of them?

Did you have a favorite uncle or aunt?
What do you best remember about them?

Which of your neighbors were memorable?
What stories do you remember about them?

How did you meet your spouse?
What made you decide to marry him/her?

What:

What are your most vivid childhood memories?

What was the most serious illness you had as a child?

What do you remember best about your grade school years?

What did you do as a child that got you in the most trouble?
How did your parents handle it?

What were your mother's best and worst traits?
Which of these traits do you share with your mother?

What were your father's best and worst traits?
Which of these traits do you share with your father?

What do you remember best about your brothers and sisters?
In what ways did they influence your growing up years?
What stories do you remember about things you did with them?

What activities did you love most in high school?

What do you remember about your first real romance?

What: (continued)

What was your most embarrassing moment?

What things do you enjoy doing today that you also enjoyed in your youth?

What things do your remember about being a teenager?

What was important to you then—dreams, goals, etc.?

What family traditions do you still remember?

What holidays were special in your family?
What did you do to celebrate them?

What do you remember about your first job?
How much did you make and how did you spend your money?

What events most changed your life?

Where:

Where did you live as a child?

Why:

Was religion important in your home?
If so, what practices made it important?

Was higher education important to you?
If so, what educational experiences were pivotal in your life?

How did you decide what to study?
How did you choose your vocation and how have you liked it?

How many jobs have you had and which did you like most? Least?

When:

Was junior high a hard transition time?

Chart #1 –Personal Profile

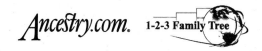

Full Name: _____

Birth Date: _____

Birth Place: _____

_____

_____

Religious Events: _____

_____

_____

_____

_____

Education: _____

_____

_____

_____

_____

Marriage: _____

_____

_____

Children: _____

_____

_____

_____

Miscellaneous: _____

_____

_____

_____

_____

_____

_____

_____

_____

_____

Chart #2 –Parents and Grandparents Information

Mother's Name: _____

Father's Name: _____

Mother's Birth Place: _____

Birth Date: _____

Father's Birth Place: _____

Birth Date: _____

Parent's Marriage Information*: _____

Parent's Death Information*: _____

Miscellaneous: _____

Grandmother's Name: _____

Grandfather's Name: _____

Grandmother's Birth Place: _____

Birth Date: _____

Grandfather's Birth Place: _____

Birth Date: _____

Grandparent's Marriage Information*: _____

Grandparent's Death Information*: _____

Miscellaneous: _____

* if applicable

©MyFamily.com, Inc. 2002

Chart #3 –Living Source List

1. _____

2. _____

3. _____

4. _____

5. _____

6. _____

7. _____

8. _____

9. _____

10. _____

11. _____

12. _____

13. _____

14. _____

15. _____

16. _____

17. _____

18. _____

19. _____

20. _____

Chart #4 – Correspondence Record

Family _____   Researcher _____

Date Sent	Addressee/Address	Purpose	Date Replied	Results

Ancestry.com.

1-2-3 Family Tree

Form # F105

©MyFamily.com, Inc. 2002

Chart #5 –Research Calendar

Family _____   Researcher _____

Date	Repository Call # Microfilm #	Description of Source	Time Period/ Names Searched	Results

Ancestral Chart

No. 1 on this chart is
the same person as No. _____

On Chart No. _____

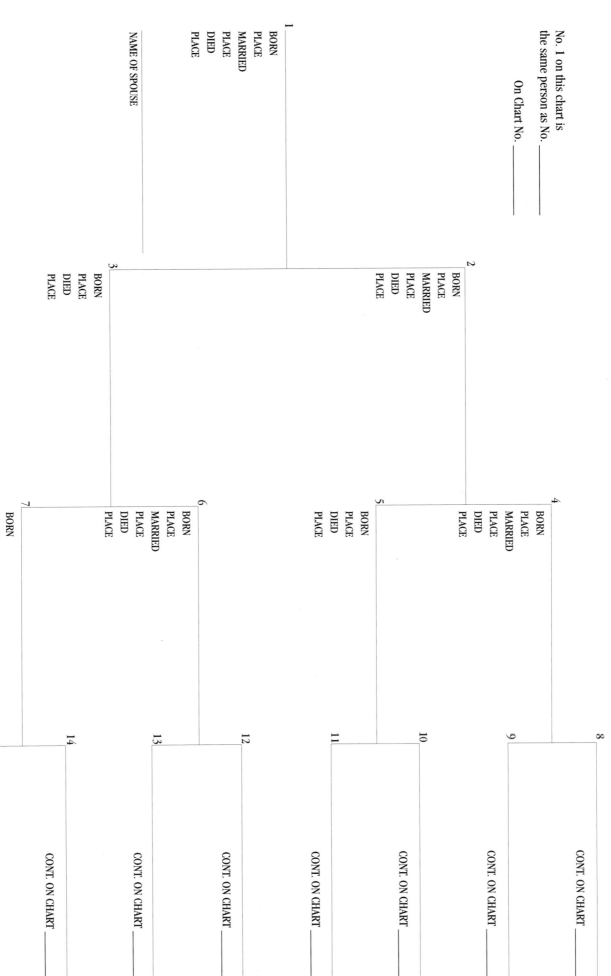

1

BORN
PLACE
MARRIED
PLACE
DIED
PLACE

NAME OF SPOUSE

2

BORN
PLACE
MARRIED
PLACE
DIED
PLACE

3

BORN
PLACE
DIED
PLACE

4

BORN
PLACE
MARRIED
PLACE
DIED
PLACE

5

BORN
PLACE
DIED
PLACE

6

BORN
PLACE
MARRIED
PLACE
DIED
PLACE

7

BORN
PLACE
DIED
PLACE

8

CONT. ON CHART _____

9

CONT. ON CHART _____

10

CONT. ON CHART _____

11

CONT. ON CHART _____

12

CONT. ON CHART _____

13

CONT. ON CHART _____

14

CONT. ON CHART _____

15

CONT. ON CHART _____

Form # F120

www.ancestry.com/save/charts/ancchart.htm

©MyFamily.com, Inc. 2002

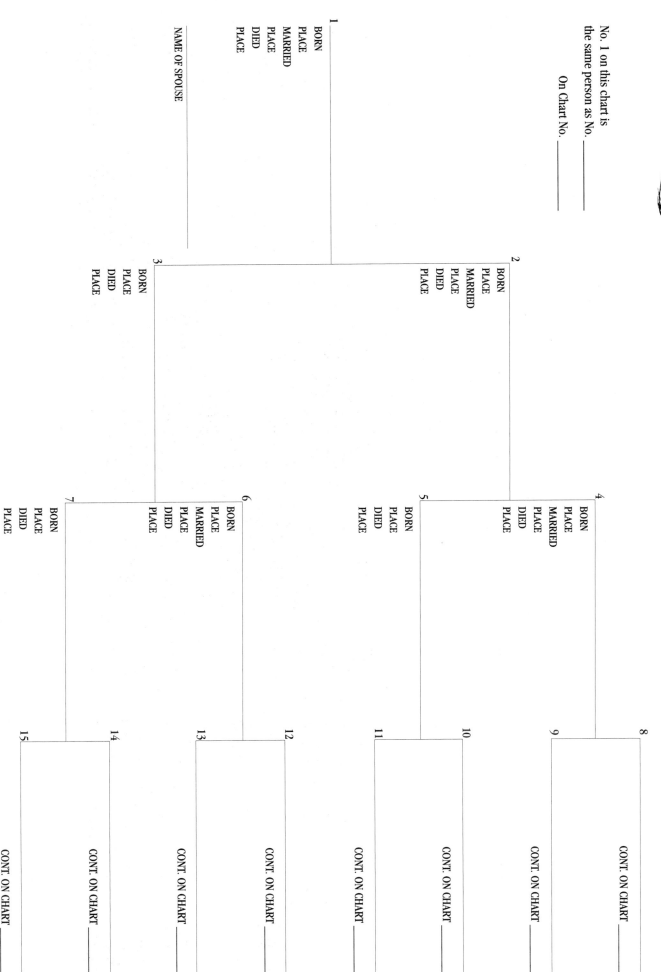

Ancestry.com.

1-2-3 Family Tree

Ancestral Chart

Chart No. _____

No. 1 on this chart is
the same person as No. _____

On Chart No. _____

1 _____

BORN
PLACE
MARRIED
PLACE
DIED
PLACE

NAME OF SPOUSE

2 _____

BORN
PLACE
MARRIED
PLACE
DIED
PLACE

3 _____

BORN
PLACE
DIED
PLACE

4 _____

BORN
PLACE
MARRIED
PLACE
DIED
PLACE

5 _____

BORN
PLACE
DIED
PLACE

6 _____

BORN
PLACE
MARRIED
PLACE
DIED
PLACE

7 _____

BORN
PLACE
DIED
PLACE

8 _____

CONT. ON CHART _____

9 _____

CONT. ON CHART _____

10 _____

CONT. ON CHART _____

11 _____

CONT. ON CHART _____

12 _____

CONT. ON CHART _____

13 _____

CONT. ON CHART _____

14 _____

CONT. ON CHART _____

15 _____

CONT. ON CHART _____

Notes

Notes

_____

_____

_____

_____

_____

_____

_____

_____

_____

_____

_____

_____

_____

_____